Occupy

A 30 DAY DEVOTIONAL

BY: JOIE MILLER

Published in Canonsburg, PA by Champion Center Publishing.

Scripture quotations marked (NIV) are taken from the Holy Bible, New International Version®, NIV®. Copyright © 1973, 1978, 1984, 2011 by Biblica, Inc.™ Used by permission of Zondervan. All rights reserved worldwide. www.zondervan.com The "NIV" and "New International Version" are trademarks registered in the United States Patent and Trademark Office by Biblica, Inc.™

Scripture quotations marked (NLT) are from the Holy Bible, New Living Translation, copyright © 1996, 2004, 2007, 2013, 2015 by Tyndale House Foundation. Used by permission of Tyndale House Publishers Inc., Carol Stream, Illinois 60188. All rights reserved.

Scripture quotations marked (ESV) are from The Holy Bible, English Standard Version® (ESV®), copyright © 2001 by Crossway, a publishing ministry of Good News Publishers. Used by permission. All rights reserved.

Scripture quotations marked (AMP) are taken from the Amplified® Bible (AMP), Copyright © 2015 by The Lockman Foundation. Used by permission. www.lockman.org

Scripture marked (MSG) taken from The Message® Bible, Copyright © 1993, 1994, 1995, 1996, 2000, 2001, 2002. Used by permission of NavPress Publishing Group.

ISBN 978-1-7360420-4-5

Introduction

"Occupy until I come."
Luke 19:13 KJV

Luke 19:13 is a directive Jesus uses in a parable referring to a master and his servants. The parable Jesus taught is widely known as the parable of the talents. Jesus reminds us of this parable as an instruction on how to steward our lives on earth until His return.

The word occupy refers to the idea of stewardship over our lives, carefully utilizing our God-given resources, time, and talents for the Kingdom of God. We are to be about our Father's business until He returns for His reward. To occupy is to fill in a void of some kind. As Christians, we will occupy our time until Christ's return in some way or another. Some of us will occupy the void with meaningless pleasures or even selfish ambition. Some of us will hide our talents for fear of man, fear of failure, or worse yet; some may be lulled to sleep by life, sitting on the talents, giftings, and time that God has allotted us on the earth to take ground for the Kingdom.

The parable in Luke 19 reminds us that we all have a responsibility to faithfully use what God has given us on earth, to which we will be called to give an account. 1 Corinthians 15:57-58 says, "But thanks be to God, who gives us the victory through our Lord Jesus Christ. Therefore, my beloved brethren, be steadfast, immovable, always abounding in the work of the Lord, knowing that your labor is not in vain in the Lord.".

As we occupy this year, 1 Corinthians 15 reminds us that we are to be steadfast, firm, and unmovable in our Hope of the return of our Master.

While we remain steadfast and occupied, we are not swayed by the world around us. Our mind and mission are fixed on Jesus and the advancement of His Kingdom. He has given us all authority on earth until His return (Lk 10:19). We are His ambassadors, doing His work. This is a time to occupy and take ground like never before!

I pray you walk in the revelation that everywhere your feet step is ground to take for the Kingdom of God. Jesus will return, and we will give an account of how we have stewarded our lives. Let's long to hear the words, " Well done, my good and faithful servant." There is work to do in your family, your workplace, and whatever realm you influence. There is always a space to occupy for the Kingdom! Let's advance like never before. On earth as it is in Heaven! Let's occupy!

"Build houses and settle down; plant gardens and eat what they produce. Marry and have sons and daughters; find wives for your sons and give your daughters in marriage, so that they too may have sons and daughters."
Jeremiah 29:5-7 NIV

Day 1

Have you ever gone somewhere and the host tells you to take your shoes and coat off and get comfortable? This is very inviting except when you don't plan to stay long. Maybe you were returning a book or dropping off a dinner, and you had somewhere else to be. Or perhaps you're an introvert, and the thought of committing to visit longer than a few minutes terrifies you. The idea of taking your shoes off and staying awhile is precisely what God was saying to the Israelites in Jeremiah 29:5-7. The Israelites had just gone into captivity. In their minds, this captivity wouldn't last very long, so they didn't want to get comfortable in this foreign place. They didn't want to unpack their things for any declaration of permanence. They were just going to hunker down and survive. They were in survival mode.

While the children of God were waiting for their deliverance, God had another idea for their time in a foreign land. God didn't want them just to survive, although they were in a season and a place that they didn't like. He wanted them to occupy the land. God wanted them to operate in the blessing, even though the conditions weren't ideal.

"HE ALWAYS WANTS US TO THRIVE, EVEN WHEN THE CIRCUMSTANCES AREN'T IDEAL."

Maybe you are in a season of life where the conditions aren't ideal. Maybe it's a season of change or transition, or maybe you're in a valley, and circumstances are so dire that you are just trying to get through. God never wants His children to just get through or maintain. He always wants us to thrive, even when the circumstances aren't ideal.

In Jeremiah, God communicated that life shouldn't stop because they were uncomfortable. They should continue to occupy, take over, and produce. They were to multiply and establish a life of blessing.

God has called us to be in this world, but not of it. That means this world may bring difficult times, and you may even be tempted to adapt to a Christianity that just holds tight until Jesus comes. But you are not of this world. That means that the blessing on your life is not bound to the perfect conditions of comfort. You are blessed by God. Allow a space for that blessing to flow. Take the lid off of what you want or think you should do to maintain or survive in this season. Build, plant, multiply, produce!

God is calling you to make a mark for His glory where you're at now, not one day when everything is perfect. Your blessing is now, your joy is now, your fruitfulness is now—in this season! So, enter this season with a mindset of occupying, not just surviving, and see what God will do!

— A DECLARATION FOR TODAY —

I will stay focused on the vision God has given me so that I am ready to run with it!

Journal:

What areas have you been surviving in which you can step out in faith to thrive and multiply?

_____

_____

_____

_____

_____

_____

_____

_____

_____

_____

_____

_____

"And whatever you do, in word or deed, do everything in the name of the Lord Jesus, giving thanks to God the Father through him."
Colossians 3:17 ESV

Day 2

How would you define a purposeful life? It's easy to compartmentalize purpose to spiritual things. So many times, I have witnessed people who get on fire for God and immediately quit their jobs or change careers because they want a greater purpose. Sometimes, people are called out of secular jobs to pursue full-time ministry, but most times, God calls us to fulfill our purpose through our work. In this case, God isn't calling a person out of what they are doing to fulfill their purpose; rather, they are bringing a greater purpose to what they are doing already.

For example, our kids all attend public school. Even though I always thought our children would attend private school, the Lord directed us to the public system. One of the values we've tried to instill into them is that the school is their mission field. We've tried to teach them that there is Kingdom purpose wherever they are and whatever they do. They are not just going about life living for themselves; they are stewarding everything they do for the Kingdom of God.

> "WHETHER YOU BAG GROCERIES, WORK AT A BUSINESS, ARE A TEACHER, A NURSE, OR A STAY-AT-HOME MOM, YOU HAVE A PURPOSE— YOU ARE A MINISTER OF THE GOSPEL!"

If every Christian assumes that being saved and on fire for God equates to serving full time on a church staff, we are forfeiting our Kingdom influence. You're an ambassador of Christ wherever you set your feet.

Even though I have always sensed a call to full-time ministry, I went through times when it felt like my purpose was set on a shelf. The contrary was true; some of my life's most fruitful seasons were when I was at home taking care of my kids. If I were measuring ministry, what seemed like the least productive times became some of my most fruitful. I didn't wait for the ministry to validate my purpose. I would go door to door in my neighborhood, asking the women to join me for snacks and a Bible study in my living room. Wow! God did some amazing things. I didn't wait for my purpose; I began living it for the glory of God. Not only was I raising up Godly kids, but I was seeing my neighbors come alive to the hope of Jesus! Everything I was doing in that season was for Jesus.

Stop waiting for your purpose to be validated through a ministry position or a spiritual title. Start living out Colossians 3:17. Whatever you do, do everything in the name of the Lord! When you start living through this lens, your life has a new purpose. Whether you are bagging groceries, working at a business, a teacher, a nurse, or a stay-at-home mom— you have a purpose; you are a minister of the gospel! Begin looking at life as your mission field, and see God use you like never before!

A DECLARATION FOR TODAY

My life is a mission field. I do everything in the name of the Lord Jesus Christ!

Journal:

What would you define as a purposeful life? Journal a list of things that make you feel like you have purpose.

_____

_____

_____

_____

_____

_____

_____

_____

_____

_____

_____

_____

Day 3

Have you ever driven in the fog? I was driving through the mountains with my kids to a lacrosse tournament, and we hit a dense patch of fog. This was possibly the most hazardous condition I have ever driven in. My visibility was impaired entirely, yet I had to keep moving. The fog was so dense that I couldn't even see what was to the right or left of me to pull over. My only option was to move forward one small increment at a time. As the headlights illuminated small distances, I could only see what was directly in front of me. Even though I preferred full visibility, this was enough to make progress.

Walking out God's plan can often feel like driving in fog. Stepping out in faith can be scary. How do you know what you are doing is going to work? What if you didn't hear from God but just ate too much pizza before bed and had a weird dream that you thought was God? First steps can be the hardest, yet they are the most necessary for progression. Studies show that if you wait until you are 100% sure of something before you move on it, you won't act because the most assurance you will usually get on big decisions is 80%.

"HE WILL POUR THE LIGHT OF HIS FAVOR ON YOU AND BLESS THE WORK OF YOUR HANDS!"

The other 20% is a step of faith, faith despite unknown factors that can catch you by surprise or present challenges. You are making the right decision when God is in the 20%.

The first steps require faith; starting something requires faith. Zechariah 4:10 reminds our hearts, "Do not despise these small beginnings, for the Lord rejoices to see the work begin." God gets happy when we start something because we are exercising faith!

God's Word illuminates our path, even when it shows us small increments forward. His peace is our guide when we can't see what's on either side of us.

Take courage today that no matter how scary your first steps forward may feel, you are not alone! God is with you; you will not fail! Step out and give God something to bless. God can't direct a parked car. Start moving in the illumination that He has given you, as small as it may seem—and you will begin to see His blessing! He will pour the light of His favor on you and bless the work of your hands!

I will step out in faith, knowing God illuminates my path; He is always with me!

Journal:

What are the small steps of obedience you can begin to take to show God that you are willing to start?

"Ask and it will be given to you; seek and you will find; knock and the door will be opened to you. For everyone who asks receives; the one who seeks finds; and to the one who knocks; the door will be opened."
Matthew 7:7-8 NIV

Day 4

How assertive are you when it comes to asking for what you want? On the assertive chart, I don't rate very high. For as long as I can remember, I have been shy when asking others for things. This was especially true with my father. I don't know why this was; he wanted to say yes to almost anything I wanted. Maybe it was my personality, fear of rejection, thinking I hadn't earned a request, or just plain fear of being told no – whatever the reason was, I noticed this carried over into my prayer life. As I grew in my faith, I realized that if I wanted something or saw Biblically what could be mine, I had to go after it in faith.

There is an assertiveness that the Bible refers to in our prayers in Matthew 7:7-8, "Ask and it will be given to you; seek and you will find; knock and the door will be opened to you. For everyone who asks receives; the one who seeks finds; and to the one who knocks; the door will be opened." This verse tells us that when it comes to prayer, I have permission from God to go after that, which I believe Him for.

"I REALIZED THAT IF I WANTED SOMETHING, OR SAW BIBLICALLY WHAT COULD BE MINE, I HAD TO GO AFTER IT IN FAITH."

When your prayer life goes from passive to assertive, everything changes. There is a new boldness that doesn't offend God but actually pleases Him! Hebrews 4:16 tells us we are to "boldly approach the throne of grace."

Boldness is the opposite of being passive. Passive prayers sound nice, but God wants us to pray with confidence. This confidence doesn't come from our righteousness but from understanding our righteousness in Christ. Not in an arrogant manner, but we should pray with boldness because of the price that Jesus paid to give us access to every promise found in the Word of God! If God said it in His Word, He wants me to go after what He said was already mine in prayer. Passive prayer stops at asking. As a child, I sometimes thought God might be angry with me, so I hesitated to ask for things. I worried that I had done something to disqualify my requests or that I might offend God. It's the mentality of, I asked, and nothing happened. God tells us in Matthew 7 that after we ask, keep asking. After we seek, keep seeking. And then... knock and keep knocking!

Whatever you believe God for, do not give up! If He spoke it in His word, it's a promise for you! Get bold in your prayer life, and take things to the next level, not because we deserve it in our own righteousness but because Jesus already paid the price!

— A DECLARATION FOR TODAY —

I will pray bold prayers and take my prayer life to the next level!

Journal:

What areas do you need to get more bold in your prayers? Write down scriptures that back up what you are believing God for!

_____.

_____

_____

_____

_____

_____

_____

_____

_____

_____

_____

_____

_____

_____

_____

Day 5

"This is the day the Lord has made. We will rejoice and be glad in it" (Psalm 118:24). I often wonder what kind of mood the psalmist was in when he wrote this psalm. This is the verse I usually wake my kids up with. Before they even get out of bed, I remind them that the day's tone isn't determined by which side of the bed they wake up on—having a good day begins with a decision.

I would love to think that the psalm writer was having a great day as he penned Psalm 118, but maybe he wasn't. Could he have possibly been redirecting his focus and mood when he declared, "I will rejoice"? It is written almost as a declaration to himself. The book of Psalms is one of the most relatable books of the Bible. Through it, we get a glimpse into the raw emotions of the psalmist. Some psalms are happy, while some are somber. I love seeing the literary shift when the psalmist gets in his feelings in a way that takes him out of faith. There is a visible shift in the tone. One of my favorite shifts is in Psalm 43:5. David is being real before God. He is taking a moment to lament over his situation. Which, by the way, is okay to do.

"GIVE YOUR FEELINGS TO GOD, THEN LEARN TO GO INTO FAITH MODE."

God knows everything, so putting on your "I'm fine" face with God is silly. Faith isn't hiding your emotions; it's confronting them with the truth of who God is!

Even though God has made you with human emotions, they don't have to dictate your life. Give your feelings to God, then learn to go into faith mode. David learned to encourage himself. He proclaims, "Why, my soul, are you downcast? Put your hope in God, for I will yet praise Him" (Psalm 43:5). After David's lamentation, he snaps himself out of his pity party and redirects his emotions to magnify God. One of the best things you can do is to become your own source of encouragement. You are a child of God. That means you are no longer dictated primarily by how you feel but by the hope in Jesus. If you constantly magnify your problems, your soul will be downcast, sad, and funky. When you speak to your emotions to magnify the Lord, everything shifts! You realize you can have joy and peace through whatever happens. You don't have to wait for the perfect day or perfect feelings- you can access them now!

Our emotions don't have to lead us. Make a daily decision to rejoice. Whether on the mountain or traveling through the valley, every day is the day the Lord has made. Each day has its own reasons to give Him praise. Make a decision to rejoice today. Redirect your emotions and magnify the Lord! Today is a good day to have a good day!

— A DECLARATION FOR TODAY —

This is the day the Lord has made. I will rejoice and be glad in it.

Journal:

Direct your heart in gladness. Construct a joy journal entry. What are 5-10 things that bring you joy in your life?

_____

_____

_____

_____

_____

_____

_____

_____

_____

_____

"As each has received a gift, use it to serve one another, as good stewards of God's varied grace."

1 Peter 4:10 ESV

Day 6

We have a family of seven, so our household can get very messy, very quickly. Many days, I've found myself frustrated by a mess saying things like, "If everyone would just do their part, things would flow so much easier." When I am the one carrying the weight of the household, it becomes too much to bear. A healthy and functional home requires contribution from everyone! No chore is so small that it's not helpful when someone pitches in.

God's house runs similarly to a family household. There are no spectators in God's family. We are all participants. In the Kingdom, we can minimize our gift or the grace upon our lives. We may feel our gift is not noticed or necessary, so why use it? God's family was never meant to be built around a few key players. Each of us has a special or unique calling that may seem small, but it can only be fulfilled by the one who has it. Another way the Bible illustrates this point is through the human body. We are the body of Christ, each with a valuable part to play. 1 Corinthians 12:12-20 reminds us that each member or part of the human body has a function; without it, the body would not function to full capacity.

"THERE IS NOTHING ORDINARY ABOUT THE UNIQUE GIFT GOD HAS ON YOUR LIFE."

Each is unique yet important. Holding back this grace in our lives robs the entire body or family of believers of its contribution. Just like our children are all good at different things, each one is equally loved and valued by us as their parents. Our family wouldn't be what it is without each member.

Often, we diminish our grace because we take it for granted. If something comes easy to us, it is a gift. We can assume what we're graced for is also easy for everyone else, making us feel ordinary. There is nothing ordinary about the unique gift God has on your life. Your grace is necessary to see the full call of the family of God flourish. Your call is never just about you-it's much bigger than just you. It takes each one of us taking our place to see God's will fully come forth in the earth! Others need your grace. Take the story of the construction, for example:

A man was walking by the construction site of a massive building. He stopped and asked three men what they were building. The first man responded, "A sidewalk." The second man said, "A parking lot." The third man mixing concrete responded, "We are building a great cathedral."

The third man saw a vision bigger than his concrete contribution. He saw something great and beyond what he could do alone. This is how we should view our gift to the body of Christ.

— A DECLARATION FOR TODAY —

My gift and grace are necessary to the family of God. My call is not just about me.

19

Journal:

Journal an aspect of your grace that is bigger than you.

_____

_____

_____

_____

_____

_____

_____

_____

_____

_____

_____

_____

_____

> "And the Lord answered me: 'Write the vision; make it plain on tablets, so he may run who reads it.'"
> Habakkuk 2:2 ESV

Day 7

Have you ever tried to get somewhere without directions? I don't know how I survived before Google Waze and Maps. We don't have strong internet service at our house, so I will often sit at the bottom of my driveway waiting for some response from my phone as to whether I should turn left or right from my house. I know it's kind of pathetic, but that's how much I rely on directions! I want to know which way to go and the most efficient way to get there. In Habakkuk 2:2, God is giving us insight into what to do with the information He gives us. It reads, "And the Lord answered me: 'Write the vision; make it plain on tablets, so he may run who reads it.'" God had given a vision to His people for a purpose– advancement! God still speaks to His children. He gives us visions that can come in all kinds of packages- an impression in your spirit where you just know what you are supposed to do, a word delivered from another saint that is confirmed in your spirit, or a desire put in you by God that comes out as a dream or aspiration. Whatever way God speaks to us, He wants us to take action. So many times, Christians will hear from God and never move forward. Often, they will say things like, "I'm just waiting on God." But maybe God is waiting on them.

"WHATEVER WAY GOD SPEAKS TO US, HE WANTS US TO TAKE ACTION."

When God speaks to you, write it down and make it plain! Writing things down shows God that you take seriously what He has spoken. If you were in the company of a great leader, hopefully, you would write down any advice they gave you. How much more so with the God of the universe speaking directly to you? Start by journaling your prayer time: What did you take before God? How did He respond to you? Did you feel a scripture drop into your spirit? Did you feel peace or clarity about a particular situation? Take time to paraphrase from your journaling a specific theme or direction God is giving you. Trust me, this exercise may feel weird at first, but as you start habitually journaling (do whatever fits your personality; there's no right or wrong way to journal), you will have a clearer picture of what God is speaking to you.

Then, make it plain. Simplify what God is speaking in two to three sentences. As you take time to put what you perceive He is saying into words, even more clarity will come. From that, clarity springs forth action. Action can be expressed through simple steps of obedience, or maybe your action is just to trust God daily. Whatever action steps emerge, it's an opportunity to move forward in the areas you may feel stuck. Maybe there are questions or prayers that you have been praying for, but you don't know what to do next. Writing down what God is speaking and taking time to perceive what you have written will propel you forward in your relationship with God. Journaling will help you get unstuck in your prayer time and your life.

A DECLARATION FOR TODAY

I am a child of God; I hear His voice clearly and consistently.

Journal:

Write down what God has been speaking to you and make it plain. Turn what God is saying into action steps, even if your action step is to continue to stand in faith!

_____

_____

_____

_____

_____

_____

_____

_____

_____

_____

_____

Day 8

Has anyone ever given you something to watch over? Like a friend who uses the restroom and asks you to look after her purse or, more importantly, her child. I take it very seriously when someone puts me in charge of something to watch over or guard. No matter how small or large the thing is, I can't rest until it's safely back in the care of its owner. 2 Timothy 1:14 reminds us that we are to guard or diligently watch over the treasure entrusted to us. The treasure God is speaking of through Paul is the treasure of truth. The truth revealed to our hearts once we receive Jesus Christ is a rare treasure. We are challenged to guard the revelation that our heart finds with all fierceness and diligence. If we keep the truth, the truth will keep us. As we guard truth through the indwelling work of the Holy Spirit, the Spirit who is truth strengthens our soul. As the treasure of truth is guarded, the value of its work begins to penetrate to the depths of our being, which brings life-altering transformation. Therefore, This treasure becomes more precious with every work it does for us—much too precious to forfeit. And the work that it takes for our souls to be transformed is much too long-suffering to take lightly.

"IF WE KEEP THE TRUTH,
THE TRUTH WILL KEEP US."

How do we allow the Holy Spirit to help us guard God's work in our hearts as trusted vessels?

First, we should continue to seek out truth. Like a rare diamond or jewel, truth has many different sides, each one more brilliant and containing more depth. The more you understand truth, the more you want to understand it. Be a student of the Word, continuing to store its treasure in your heart. When you read the Bible, ask Holy Spirit to illuminate truth to you.

Second, cultivate or maintain truth. Allow the Holy Spirit to help you apply truth to your heart and life. James reminds us that faith without action is dead. Truth, although guarded as a treasure, shouldn't remain hidden. It should shine forth from your life. Lastly, live in it. As you allow the Spirit of Truth (Holy Spirit) to help you cultivate the gift of God in you, allow truth to penetrate your soul. The soul cannot reach its full capacity of happiness and contentment outside of truth, so enjoy the benefit of the treasure you are entrusted to carry!

—— A DECLARATION FOR TODAY ——

I will be a student of the Word and continue to store its treasure in my heart.

Journal:

List three ways the Holy Spirit is doing a work in your heart right now.

_____

_____

_____

_____

_____

_____

_____

_____

_____

_____

_____

_____

"Set your minds on things above, not on earthly things."
Colossians 3:2 NIV

Day 8

There is great power in perspective. For example, the old question, "Is the glass half full or half empty?" The glass has the same amount of water; how you view it determines if it is closer to being full or empty. Colossians 3:2 gives us some advice on how to live our lives from a half-full perspective. It says, "Set your minds on things above, not on earthly things." We tend to focus our attention on the earthly things around us, such as car payments, career goals, and why our kids aren't acting like our neighbor's kids- all of the things that fight for our attention every day.

When we focus on these things, they become our gods. We begin to worry, compare, complain, and strive for the things of this earth. What we meditate on is magnified in our lives. Earthly things start to dictate our joy, peace, and faith. We become double-minded in our thinking, focused on God one minute and focused on our natural situations the next. The book of James tells us that this type of thinking creates "a double-mindedness in which we should expect to receive nothing from God." (James 1:8). So how do you keep your focus set on the things above? We live in the world. We are not of it, but we are indeed in it.

"WHAT WE MEDITATE ON IS MAGNIFIED IN OUR LIVES."

That means we have to intentionally keep our focus and affection on Him. One of the best ways to keep our perspective clear is through thanksgiving and praise. The Bible tells us to enter His gates with thanksgiving and His courts with praise (Psalm 100:4). Our perspective shifts when we begin to offer thanksgiving and praise. No longer do the things of earth seem so big or even important. The reality of the majesty of our God transcends any worry or care of this world.

Simply put, when God becomes bigger, the cares of life become small. As we lift God up, we are not only worshipping our God but also reminding ourselves who the God we serve is. In the place of praise and thanksgiving, our faith begins to rise! What once seemed impossible in your life will feel easy through faith. The more you praise, the less you will complain. Just as thanksgiving attracts God, complaining and unbelief repel Him.

Take a few moments today and lift up the name of the Lord. Set your mind on Him, not on your situation. As you do, you will enter a new perspective of supernatural peace and joy and begin to ask yourself questions like, "If God is for me, who or what could be against me?" Change your perspective, and your entire life will change! Set your eyes upon Jesus, and like the old hymn states, "And the things of earth will become strangely dim in the light of His glorious face."

— A DECLARATION FOR TODAY —

I will set my focus on the things above, not on earthly things.

Take a few minutes and magnify the Lord. Set your mind on Him—not your worries, not your to-do list, just on Him. Journal how you feel at the end of your praise session!

_____

_____

_____

_____

_____

_____

_____

_____

_____

_____

_____

_____

"Enlarge the place of your tent, and let the curtains of your habitations be stretched out; do not hold back; lengthen your cords and strengthen your stakes."
Isaiah 54:2 ESV

Day 10

Stretching is uncomfortable. Not too long ago, I hurt my back on a trip. Usually, when I am in pain, I just endure until it goes away. However, this time, the pain reached a level of discomfort that I could no longer ignore. Before going to a doctor, I implemented everything I knew to do. I started by stretching my back a few times a day. At first, specific stretches were extremely uncomfortable yet relieving. The more I stretched, the less pain I felt. Stretching solved the problem! It turns out that my back got stiff from staying in one position for too long on an airplane. What a metaphor for life. As we navigate through life, it is easy to become comfortable in one position, or season instead, for so long that we don't realize it's crippling us. It's not until staying the same becomes more painful than moving forward that we welcome the stretch in our lives. Stretch seasons are necessary for growth. Isaiah 54:2 says, "Enlarge the place of your tent, and let the curtains of your habitations be stretched out; do not hold back; lengthen your cords and strengthen your stakes." When we take ground in our lives, there is always a level of discomfort that takes us from what has always been into what God wants us to obtain.

"HE NEVER WANTS YOU TO DIMINISH, BUT TO INCREASE IN EVERY AREA."

Growth is necessary. The reward is always worth it, but the process is often painful. Stretching at first feels more harmful than beneficial. Seasons of growth can often appear as loss or shrinking back. Nothing is more frustrating than desiring to move forward while feeling like you are in reverse. When you start to embrace growth, you value the stretching process. Stretching uses tension to make something expand. When you stretch, you reach new levels that, after time, become your new norm.

What area do you discern God is asking you to stretch in? God desires for your tent to be enlarged so that you can take more ground in the area of your influence and domain. This is uncomfortable at times. This type of growth can challenge you to the core. Maybe the pain or discomfort of this season is a catalyst for the stretch.

Push past the discomfort, push past the desire to hold on to what was or is, and commit to stretching and being flexible to what God wants to do next. He never wants you to diminish but to increase in every area!

A DECLARATION FOR TODAY

Every season is my best season with the Lord!

Journal:

Journal about the stretch. What areas of growth are you being called to?

_____

_____

_____

_____

_____

_____

_____

_____

_____

_____

_____

_____

"But as it is written, 'What no eye has seen, nor ear heard, nor heart of man imagined, what God has prepared for those who love Him.'"
1 Corinthians 2:9 ESV

Day 11

Have you ever been in a situation where someone tried to explain something to you, but you couldn't understand? Maybe it was a new concept or way of doing something, or the idea was so big that it was just too hard to imagine. Possibly, the idea or concept was just out of your mind, out of the realm of possibility. The Bible tells us in 1 Corinthians 2:9 that God has plans for us that are so big they are hard to imagine; His plans are out of our minds. "But as it is written, 'What no eye has seen, nor ear heard, nor heart of man imagined, what God has prepared for those who love Him." While God's plans for us may be too big to understand fully, we must get a glimpse of them through faith and start to imagine the God-sized possibilities for our lives. We will never obtain it if we can't see it in our imaginations. First, we see by faith, not by natural sight. Hebrews 11:1 says, "Now faith is the confidence in what we hope for and the assurance about what we do not see." If you can easily imagine God's plan for you, you are probably not imagining big enough. God's plan will always stretch us past the point of possibility and capability. If you can accomplish God's plan on your own, it doesn't require faith.

"IF YOU CAN ACCOMPLISH GOD'S PLAN ON YOUR OWN, IT DOESN'T REQUIRE FAITH."

Through faith, we live a life full of God-sized fulfillment.

Take a minute to think about Abraham. God had a conversation with Abraham about the plans and purpose for his life. In Genesis, God reveals to Abraham that he will have a son. Immediately, Abraham starts to rationalize with God. In Genesis 15:3, Abraham responds to God's plan by saying, "A servant in my household will be my heir." Abraham could not imagine the possibility that he and Sarah would have a child of their own. It was beyond what Abraham labeled possible; he couldn't see what God communicated. In verse 5, God makes His plan clear to Abraham. "He took him outside and said, 'Look up at the sky and count the stars-if indeed you can count them.'" Then He said to him, "So shall your offspring be" (Genesis 15:5). Abraham couldn't even conceive the idea of having one heir, while God was thinking way beyond one son. He was thinking of nations!

What plans does God have for you that you have dismissed because you can't conceive that He could do them through you? What promises are you trying to rationalize in the realm of your capacity to accomplish them? God has so much more for you. More than you can ask, think, or imagine in your own ability. Activate your faith today. Stop putting God in a box and start looking up to the heavens. Take the limits off of God's plan for you and ask Him for eyes of faith to see what He sees for you, then dare to believe it!

A DECLARATION FOR TODAY

I have the mind of Christ - all things are possible because I believe!

Journal:

Think without limits. What are five things you would love to do if resources were not a limit?

_____

_____

_____

_____

_____

_____

_____

_____

_____

_____

_____

"Therefore, prepare your minds for action, keep sober in spirit, fix your hope completely on the grace to be brought to you at the revelation of Jesus Christ."
1 Peter 1:13 ESV

Day 12

What does it mean to be mission-minded? When I am walking through a store with a list in hand, I often tell myself to stay on mission. This means to get in, get out, and get what I need. To stick to the list without distractions. This is much easier said than done. All is good when I only look for what I came to get. The problem is when other things catch my attention. Before I know it, if I'm not diligent, my cart is full, my budget is blown, and the mission fails.

1 Peter 1:13 is a great reminder to stay on mission: "Therefore, prepare your minds for action, keep sober in spirit, fix your hope completely on the grace to be brought to you at the revelation of Jesus Christ." Like me, in any given store, life can distract us from the mission God has put before us. As a child of God, you have a very important mission- to glorify God through the gifts and blessings He has bestowed upon you. Life is too short to be anything less than mission-minded. One of the first places distraction comes is our mind. Preparing your mind for action is to stay focused on your life's purpose. Wrong mindsets or meditating on the wrong things can cause our thinking to become very temporal and fixated on earthly things.

"LIFE IS TOO SHORT TO BE ANYTHING LESS THAN MISSION-MINDED."

Earthly things are good, but they are not the ultimate mission. You are anointed and called into the Kingdom for a purpose only you can accomplish.

The enemy can put you on a side mission through distractions such as comparison and discontentment that affect your spirit in a way that robs you of joy and peace. Our spirit produces fruit by the Holy Spirit that sustains us for our God-given purpose, so we need to guard it. Galatians 5:22 tells us that the fruit of the spirit is "love, joy, peace, patience, kindness, goodness, faithfulness, gentleness, and self-control." When we allow our minds to stray from the mission, we lose the fruit God has intended to empower us for our purpose!

Stay mission-minded. Enjoy life, but don't become distracted by things tied to this world. God has created you for so much more! Shake off desires and thinking that would sabotage your ability to walk forward in your destiny. Stay ready for action, ready to take ground and move forward! Fix your eyes on Jesus; don't become sidetracked by your emotions or the actions of others. What God has in store for you is too big to get diverted by things of this life. Fill yourself with God's word daily, surround yourself with like-minded friends to encourage you to stay focused on what's truly important, and guard the fruit of the spirit to sustain and empower you to become everything God intends you to be!

— A DECLARATION FOR TODAY —

I am focused and steadfast in the good plan and purpose God has for my life.

Make a list to identify any mindsets or habits that are negatively diverting you from the mission God has called you to. Actively decide to be mission-minded!

_____

_____

_____

_____

_____

_____

_____

_____

_____

_____

_____

_____

_____

"Whatever you do, work at it with all of your heart, as working for the Lord, not for human masters."

Colossians 3:23 NIV

Day 13

Have you ever done something that you didn't want to do? As I write this, my children are helping their dad with a chore they don't really like. This can lead to a halfhearted job with the task. Don't get me wrong, when the proper motivation is involved (cash), the job gets done with less complaining and a lot more attention to detail. Colossians 3:23 reminds us that motive matters: "Whatever you do, work at it with all of your heart, as working for the Lord, not for human masters." Motivation is determined by who our master is and the why behind the what. If we look at the things we do daily absent from our God-given purpose, these things can feel meaningless and mundane.

We can get lazy in the assignments that are in front of us. When God is our master, nothing we do is meaningless. From caring for a house to taking care of children to a job that maybe isn't your dream job—with God, it has meaning. God is a God of intention. Whatever your life is comprised of at this moment, it's intentional. God is watching how we respond to His seemingly small assignments. There are things in your life right now that you may prefer not to do; do them as unto the Lord.

"MOTIVATION IS DETERMINED BY WHO OUR MASTER IS AND THE WHY BEHIND THE WHAT."

This is a lesson I've lived out in the last year. My father passed away this summer, but before he did, I spent about a year taking care of him. Days were filled with doctor appointments and caregiving. Even though I didn't love the weight of this season, I did my best to honor my father and God in all I did. Many times, doctor appointments would interrupt "ministry" appointments. Despite the temptation to become frustrated by interruptions, I did my best to steward my heart from a place where taking care of my father was my ministry in that season, and I would do it to the best of my ability. In hindsight, I am so thankful that I had the honor of caring for my dad in his final months. I could have very easily missed out on labeling what God gave me to be a blessing, as an interruption, or a burden. Trusting God with my assignment in that season wasn't only a great joy; it allowed me to be fully present in the "now" of what God was doing in and through me.

What assignment or season are you in the middle of right now? Whatever you are in the middle of, be all in. Give your best to what God has allowed you to steward this season. What may feel like a setback or an inconvenience could be a tool God is trying to use to mature or even bless you.

Trust Him today by giving your very best, not unto man but unto God!

A DECLARATION FOR TODAY

No matter the season. I give my best to God.

Journal:

Journal about your current season. What is one thing that you've been viewing as a burden that could be a blessing? How can you steward this season to the glory of God?

_____

_____

_____

_____

_____

_____

_____

_____

_____

_____

_____

> "Let us not become weary in doing good, for at the proper time we will reap a harvest of blessing if we don't give up."
> Galatians 6:9

Day 14

There is nothing like doing what's right without a reward. There have been situations in my life over and over again where I have taken the high road when I could have easily and justifiably done things differently. I'm talking about the moments when I could have defended myself or the times I could have chosen to be bitter about wrongdoing...moments where I could have gotten even. We've all been faced with the temptation to do what's easy or what feels right versus what is actually right or good. What makes doing right so difficult is that right doesn't always reap a quick reward. I often think that as soon as I make the right decision or do something contrary to what I feel like doing, I should get a pat on the back or a justice served immediately. The key to persevering in good is to do it without the reward in sight. Think about when you make a good choice in your diet. I think the moment I eat one celery stick over a cookie, I should see the scale drop. The truth is that it takes time. There is a season of *properly sowing*.

Viewing your actions as seeds fosters patience and perseverance.

"EVERY ACTION OF GOOD, EVERY CHOICE YOU MAKE FOR RIGHTEOUSNESS WILL PRODUCE A REWARD IN YOUR LIFE."

Often, the benefits of a seed emerge in ways I least expect at the moment. One time in particular, I chose to do right and forgive someone I heard was talking about me. I could have confronted this person, but instead, I chose to forgive and pray for this person. At first, I thought I would do what was right and wait for this person to get what was coming to her. The thing is, my right decision caused the right feelings to grow in my heart. Eventually, this person did reap what she had sown in a situation separate from mine. When I heard about it, my feelings shocked me. I thought this was the moment all of my "doing good" and choosing the "high road" was waiting for. A moment of justification, finally. But instead, something different happened. Upon hearing the mess that unraveled in this person's life, I wasn't happy but instead sad for her. My ability to release forgiveness reaped a harvest of love and wholeness in my heart.

Don't be discouraged today for doing good. You might feel forgotten by God or think your actions are insignificant. But be reminded today that God sees and He responds. Every action of good, every choice you make for righteousness will produce a reward in your life. Your harvest may just look and feel different than you expect! Whatever you do, don't back off from doing good—keep on keepin' on!

— A DECLARATION FOR TODAY ——————

I will be patient as I sow the right seeds, knowing they will reap a harvest in time!

What is an area of doing good that has left you frustrated? How can you change your perspective in this area?

_____

_____

_____

_____

_____

_____

_____

_____

_____

_____

_____

_____

"He who had received the five talents went at once and traded with them, and he made five talents more. So also he who has the two talents made two talents more. But he who had received the one talent went and dug it in the ground and hid his master's money."
Matthew 25: 16-30 ESV

Day 15

Have you ever been frustrated when you pray and don't get your desired answer? I once heard a story of a man praying for a table and chairs for his home. He prayed and prayed, but God never provided a table and chairs; all he was given was a tree and an axe. The gifts and talents God gives us can often be overlooked just like the man believing for a table who was given wood. Matthew 25:14 reminds us of how we are to steward our talents. We want God to hand us our destiny on a silver platter. We expect the desires of our hearts and our prayers to be answered with a big red bow around them. Often, answered prayers come in the form of good old hard work.

In the parable of the talents, the master gave each man talents to start with. It is each one's responsibility to manage and multiply what he was given. The sum of what the master expected from them was proportional to what they were given. Like the men in Matthew 25, God has given you talents and gifts. These talents are in direct proportion with your purpose. As the master with the servants, God is watching what you are doing with what He has given you.

"WHILE YOU ARE WAITING ON GOD, MAYBE HE IS WAITING ON YOU!"

Are you working your gift? Are you multiplying the things God has enabled you to use for His Kingdom? Or have you buried it, waiting for God to do all the work? Has your fear of failure or lack of self-confidence held you back from using your gift?

Each one of us is endowed for something great. Just because our talents may not all look alike, they are all equally valuable to the Kingdom. You were created on purpose for a purpose, and that purpose is yours and yours alone! Don't allow comparison to stop you from using your talent. Don't talk yourself out of multiplying your gift. Work the area God has blessed you in. Stop allowing the frustration found in the waiting to rob you of your dream. Move forward today. Everything you need to see your dream come true is already inside you– start using it.

Exercise your strengths and talents. If God has given you a gift to sing, join a worship team. If He's given you the gift of writing, start a blog. Lead a small group if you want to teach, and serve your church if you want to use your leadership skills. Just start! The answer to some of your greatest prayers could be on the other side of your obedience to step out! Don't overlook the wood and axe God has given you because it isn't a table—you make the table. While you are waiting on God, maybe He is waiting on you! Today is your day!

A DECLARATION FOR TODAY

I will exercise the strengths and talents God has given me and make my own table!

Journal:

What talents and giftings do you feel the Lord blessed you with? If you are unsure, take time with the Lord for him to reveal your special giftings to you.

_____

_____

_____

_____

_____

_____

_____

_____

_____

_____

_____

"You will keep in perfect peace those whose minds are steadfast because they trust in you."
Isaiah 26:3 NIV

Day 16

Have you ever been sitting in a church service where the Lord spoke something directly to you beyond question? Maybe it was an instruction you have been waiting on or even a seed of faith into your spirit to believe in God for something big. In that moment, the revelation you have heard from God feels so clear. But what happens when you leave service or a day or two goes by? Usually, your mind starts to question if God really spoke to you. Your mind will often talk your spirit out of the will of God.

Our minds function like computers. As soon as a thought enters our consciousness, we immediately process it as possible or impossible. If the mind deems the thought or idea as possible, it will go to work, providing supportive ideas to make it happen. If the mind deems the thought impossible, it will begin to reason in all the ways it cannot happen. The issue with this process is that when God speaks to us, He doesn't speak through our minds to see if what He says is possible, but instead, He deposits His thoughts for us in our spirit. We conceive God's promises in our spirit and then renew our minds with His Word.

"A STEADFAST MIND IS STABLE, ESTABLISHED, AND UNMOVED."

In doing this, we remind ourselves the difference between what God says is possible and what our brains tell us is possible.

Isaiah 25:3 reminds us, "You will keep in perfect peace those whose minds are steadfast because they trust in you." A steadfast mind is stable, established, and unmoved. Trusting God sets our minds that no matter what, we choose to believe God and what He has spoken to us rather than what even feels naturally possible. This type of trust produces perfect peace, the Bible says. When what God speaks feels contrary to what would be possible in the natural, perfect peace allows you to stay in a place of faith and trust.

So, the next time God speaks to your spirit, receive it by faith and then renew your mind rather than allowing your mind to judge if what God speaks is possible!

— A DECLARATION FOR TODAY —

I choose to believe God and what He has spoken rather than what feels naturally possible.

Journal:

Recount one or two times when you knew beyond a shadow of a doubt that God was speaking to you. How did your mind respond?

_____

_____

_____

_____

_____

_____

_____

_____

_____

_____

_____

_____

_____

Day 17

Have you ever wanted something so badly for someone who didn't want it themselves? There have been people in my life whom I saw potential in, yet I could not change them. I could not control their decisions to make the necessary steps to grow. Just as I can't make a plant grow by pulling on it, I couldn't cause the inside growth to happen externally. I can water the plant and create conditions for growth, but true growth originates from within. This type of growth calls for personal responsibility. Ephesians 4:7 tells us that each of us is given a grace from God. Grace given by God to us is a gift. However, it is our responsibility to grow in that grace. I could decide to stay at the same measure of grace my entire life. Would I make it to heaven? Most likely. Would I fulfill God's full measure and plan for my life? Most likely not. If you are like me, you probably desire to grow in your God-given grace. Unfortunately, desire is not enough. To grow in your grace, you need to exercise personal responsibility. Nobody can change for you. Change that brings growth is an inside job. Growing your grace can be allowing the Holy Spirit to speak to you in a way that you make choices to become like Him.

"NOBODY CAN CHANGE FOR YOU. CHANGE THAT BRINGS GROWTH IS AN INSIDE JOB."

Colossians 3:10 describes growth as "putting on the new self, which is being renewed in knowledge in the image of its Creator." Growing in your grace is growing in knowing who Jesus is and becoming more like Him each day. Sometimes, when you grow, you become less recognizable to yourself and more transformed into the best version of yourself! There have been seasons in my life where I wanted to grow so quickly that I tried to rush the process. I tried to change from the outside in. God does His best transformations from the inside out. Grace growth becomes less about striving and more about yielding to your Creator. This requires allowing the Holy Spirit to work on your heart and to say yes to each step of the growth process, even when it doesn't feel good or look pretty.

Just as growing your grace requires you to grow in the knowledge of God and to allow that knowledge to be applied to your heart, growing in grace also requires you to take personal responsibility for your gift. We have each been gifted by God for the purpose He has destined us to fulfill. Ephesians 2:10 reminds us, "We are God's workmanship, created in Christ Jesus for good works." Are you a gifted writer or a singer? As wonderful as it would be to wake up one morning and write a best-selling book or to sing a chart-breaking song, our God-gifted grace is only a starting point. It is your responsibility to grow at your gift on purpose through development and an investment of both time and sometimes finances. Although it may feel hard or require discipline, God is counting on you to develop the gift He has graced you with for your Kingdom purpose!

Make a decision today to grow. Whether it's personal growth in character or spirituality or developing a craft or gift, remember that no one else can grow for you. Growing in grace is a work only you and God can do together. No matter how hard the growth process is, it's always worth it. Allow God to start your growth process today, and then take personal responsibility to give God your yes to the process!

I will stay focused on the vision God has given me so that I am ready to run with it!

Journal:

What are areas of growth both in becoming more like Christ and in developing your grace or gift that you can recognize God calling you to?

_____

_____

_____

_____

_____

_____

_____

_____

_____

_____

_____

"For I know the plans I have for you, says the Lord. They are plans for good and not disaster, to give you a future and a hope."
Jeremiah 29:11 NLT

Day 18

I love to look at old photo albums! Reminiscing is actually something I do for fun; whether it's pictures from my childhood or when my children were babies, I love to look back over the years. As I pour over pictures, I travel down memories and emotions of the past. This is usually good, but sometimes, looking back too long can hinder us from moving forward. I have heard it said that a car has a large windshield and a small rear-view mirror for a reason. We are to spend most of our time looking forward while only reflecting back briefly. As good or as bad as past seasons have been for you, God's best is ahead. God is reminding His children of this in Jeremiah 29:11 when He says, "For I know the plans I have for you, says the Lord. They are plans for good and not disaster, to give you a future and a hope." At first glance, you may think the Israelites are receiving this promise as a word of blessing. However, God was speaking this word of encouragement to them in a time of difficulty. For the children of God, it looked like their best season was behind them. It seemed like there was nothing good in their future while they were in exile. They may have even thought God was done with them.

"AS GOOD OR AS BAD AS PAST SEASONS HAVE BEEN FOR YOU, GOD'S BEST IS AHEAD."

What God communicates in this passage couldn't be further from the future they were imagining. God was saying, "Your best days aren't behind you. Even though it may feel like the good ole days are long gone, I've got good things ahead." God was trying to get the Israelites to stop looking back and start looking forward. He was renewing their hope in His plan for them.

Are you like the Israelites today? Has a season of change or loss caused you to long for what's behind you rather than what's ahead? Allow your heart to receive fresh hope today that God's plan for you is good! Proverbs 4:18 reminds us that the path of the righteous gets brighter and brighter. No matter what yesterday looked like, your most prosperous days are in front of you!

Perhaps you are in a season of letting go—such as a child growing up and leaving home, the death of a parent, or a job transition. Change isn't always a bad thing. In fact, change is one of the most consistent things in life. Find hope and excitement in the one who holds your future and promises the best part of the plan is just ahead!

— A DECLARATION FOR TODAY —————

I am hopeful in God, who holds my future and promises the best part of the plan is just ahead!

List three things that you are excited for in this next season and three things you are grateful for from the past season

_____

_____

_____

_____

_____

_____

_____

_____

_____

_____

_____

_____

"Delight yourself in the Lord and He will give you the desires of your heart."
Psalm 37:4 ESV

Day 19

This past summer, we visited an amusement park as a family. My kids are all grown now, but as we walked through the park, I saw one of their favorite rides, which was in Kiddie Land. It was a driving ride where the kids drove in the front seat while the parent was in the back. They loved the feeling of independence as they would press the gas pedal and steer the wheel. What they didn't know was that the car was attached to a track. While the ride gave the illusion that they were in control of the vehicle, the reality was that they were just along for the ride as much as the parent was. I couldn't help but think this is how we must feel as we make decisions for our own lives, and God is along for the ride in the back seat. We have the illusion that we are in control, calling the shots, but as a child of God, He is silently orchestrating everything so that even if we tried to take a left turn off the path, we couldn't get too far outside His control.

What a benefit of being a child of God! Psalm 37:4 says, "Delight yourself in the Lord, and He will give you the desires of your heart." The beauty of this verse is that as I love and honor God with my life, He will give me my desires.

"DELIGHT YOURSELF IN THE LORD, COMMIT YOUR PATH TO HIM, AND REST ASSURED IT WILL BE A GOOD RIDE!"

While I think I'm calling the shots, God is the one who put those desires in my heart in the first place!

The second half of Psalm 37:4, "He will give you the desires of your heart," is actually translated from the phrase "from the Father." This means that God is the one who has placed the desires that you seek in your heart in the first place. What a freeing thought. I don't have to worry about chasing the wrong things or going down the wrong path when my motive is to please Him. He is the one in control of the car, watching me joyfully think I am driving.

Be encouraged today that as much as you think you are in control, God is leading you and guiding you every step of the way. He makes straight the path of the righteous (Isaiah 26:7). So delight yourself in the Lord, commit your path to Him, and rest assured it will be a good ride!

A DECLARATION FOR TODAY

I delight myself in the Lord and commit my path to Him, knowing He leads my every step!

Journal:

Journal some ways you have recognized God directing your path. How did things work out?

_____

_____

_____

_____

_____

_____

_____

_____

_____

_____

_____

"You will also decree a thing, and it will be established for you; So light will shine on your ways."
Job 22:28 NKJV

Day 20

Have you ever prayed to God, asking why things weren't happening like you wanted them to? I recall asking God why things weren't moving in the direction I had hoped, why it felt like there was no grace in the path I was on. He responded to my heart, "You have to give me something to bless." I began to think about what I felt God said. I hadn't stopped believing God would do what He had promised, but I had stopped speaking it out loud! Job 22:28 says, "You will also decree a thing, and it will be established for you; So light will shine on your ways." When we speak out in faith, faith is established. It's in that moment when faith takes root. You may be thinking about how words can be established. Have you ever been in an argument with someone? You're at the moment where you are so angry you want to say exactly what you are thinking despite the consequence of hurting the other person's feelings. The words are bubbling up inside of you; they travel from the depth of your stomach up your neck, and before you know it, you are so angry that you spit them out of your mouth! The moment you release the words, you instantly wish you could reel them back in. But you can't. You can apologize, but you cannot undo what has been established.

"FAITH SPEAKS, SO BEGIN TO GIVE YOUR FAITH A VOICE."

This is how it is with our faith, too. Faith speaks. Faith has a voice. Desires and prayers aren't meant to stay inside us; God wants them to be established. Faith is established through our words.

Job reminds us that something is established in the spiritual realm when we decree, and God then shines his favor on us. Our words literally give God something to bless! When God spoke to me to give Him something to bless, He wanted me to speak my faith so that He could start moving on my behalf! What promises do you truly believe with all your heart but haven't spoken out loud? Open your mouth and speak it out.

Faith speaks, so begin to give your faith a voice. As you do, things will start changing in your situation. You will begin to see God do the impossible on your behalf. He will show you which path to take and make all your plans succeed. This is what God's favor partnered with your faith does! Decree and speak out to establish the things of heaven here on earth!

— A DECLARATION FOR TODAY —

I speak out and decree in faith that which I am praying for is already established!

Journal:

What are some areas you need to see God's favor show up in your situations today? As you declare in faith, His favor is released!

_____

_____

_____

_____

_____

_____

_____

_____

_____

_____

_____

_____

Day 21

Faith is a fight. I am reminded of the boxing story about the legendary match between Robert Duran and Sugar Ray on November 25, 1980. Duran had beaten Sugar Ray just five months prior and became the World Champion. A second match was scheduled, and an overly confident Duran faced Sugar Ray, who had spent the months leading to the rematch in serious training. The match began and just a few rounds in, Ray was defeating Duran. Instead of finishing the match, Duran uttered the words that would label his career forever. He said, "No More." The World Champion, in the face of adversity, quit. Instead of finishing the match and doing his best to the end, he decided to forfeit. To this day, Robert Duran regrets the outcome of this match.

Standing in faith can feel much like a boxing match. There are moments when life "feels" like it is winning. There are rounds where it "feels" like the enemy is getting in the final punch. In these moments, it is vital to remember that faith is more than a feeling. Faith is the hope we have in Jesus coming to pass in our lives. 1 Timothy 6:12 tells us to "Fight the good fight of faith; take hold of the eternal life to which you were called."

"A FIGHT OF FAITH ISN'T A FIGHT FOR VICTORY. IT IS A FIGHT FROM A PLACE OF VICTORY."

Faith is a fight. If you believe that your faith will never be challenged, the slightest adversity will have you yelling, "No more."

In John 16:33, Jesus tells us, "In this world you will have trouble. But take heart! I have overcome the world." This life will have its share of obstacles, trials, and challenges, but those things do not have the final say. Jesus's victory paved the way for your victory over every trial. That means quitting is not an option when you feel like you keep getting knocked down. Get back up. The only way you lose in life is if you quit. Your faith is a guaranteed victory. You win, no matter what–if you don't quit! The Bible tells us what to do when we get knocked down, "For though a righteous man may fall seven times, they rise again" (Proverbs 24:16). A fight of faith isn't a fight for victory; it is a fight from a place of victory. Keep rising!

Adversity stewarded through faith brings maturity to your life. When the enemy comes to knock you down and make you feel defeated, remember who you are in Christ. You are more than a conqueror (Romans 8). Make a decision today to be stubborn in your faith. No matter what comes your way, quitting is not an option! If you get knocked down seven times, get up eight! Victory is a guarantee if you stay in the fight. The fight is fixed in your favor. You've got this!

— A DECLARATION FOR TODAY ——————

No weapon formed against me will prevail. I am more than a conqueror in Christ Jesus!

Journal:

Write out 3 scriptures that reaffirm who you are in Christ.

_____

_____

_____

_____

_____

_____

_____

_____

_____

_____

_____

_____

"If you have trapped yourself by your agreement and
are caught by what you said."
Proverbs 6:2 ESV

Day 22

Imagine watching a high-speed chase between a bank robber and a police officer. The chase finally ends with the robber against his car being handcuffed. What are the next words that come from the police officer's mouth? "You have the right to remain silent. Everything you say can and will be used against you in a court of law." The officer reads the criminal his Miranda Rights.

Proverbs 6:2 says, "If you have trapped yourself by your agreement and are caught by what you said." Just as a criminal has to be reminded that their words could become a snare or a trap that incriminates them in court, our words can become a snare to our faith. The words that come from our mouths hold power. Power to create and power to destroy. Just as God is waiting to use your words to establish faith, the enemy is waiting to use your words against you.

The enemy- who is also referred to in the Bible as the accuser of the brethren (Rev 2:10)- is like an unjust judge who wants to snare you by the words you have spoken. The enemy of your soul knows the power of what you say and will try to use it against you.

"THE WORDS THAT COME FROM OUR
MOUTHS HOLD POWER."

That's why, as believers, we need to be careful with our words.

In a moment of anger, frustration, or discouragement, guard your mouth. The psalmist in Psalm 141:3 prayed the prayer. "Put a guard over my mouth, o Lord that I might not sin against thee." The enemy is waiting to use every idle word you've spoken as a trap to keep you from progressing.

Make a decision today to live like the writer of Psalm 141, to keep a close guard over the words of your mouth. Begin to think before you speak. Don't let the emotion of the situation dictate your words. Everything you say can and will be used against you, so speak wisely!

Journal:

If you've been setting traps for yourself with your words, just simply repent! Ask God to forgive you and start speaking in faith!

_____

_____

_____

_____

_____

_____

_____

_____

_____

_____

_____

> "And I am sure of this, that he who began a good work in you will bring it to completion on the day of Jesus Christ."
> Philippians 1:6 ESV

Day 23

What does it mean to complete something? I recently had this conversation with my children. When asked to do a chore or a task, it seemed like they had gotten into the habit of defining their own "complete." I started noticing things at our house only getting about 80% finished. For example, when asked to clean their room, they got it almost clean – meaning the floor still needed to be vacuumed or the trash needed to be taken out. We laugh about this now, but it took redefining what complete is. Complete is 100% finished. Unlike my children (lol), when God begins something, He completes it. Philippians 1:6 says, "And I am sure of this, that he who began a good work in you will bring it to completion at the day of Jesus Christ." Aren't you glad God doesn't stop at 80%? God's finished work in you will come to pass. That means whatever desire, dream, or purpose God put into your heart through faith was just the beginning. He is working all things together in your life to see to the fulfillment of His plan. God works even when things feel undone, or a chapter is left as a cliffhanger. That relationship that isn't reconciled yet, that ministry that hasn't taken off yet, that health issue that isn't resolved yet... don't lose heart. If it's not good, God isn't finished working.

"HE IS WORKING ALL THINGS TOGETHER IN YOUR LIFE TO SEE TO THE FULFILLMENT OF HIS PLAN."

When God starts something, His goodness prevails. Even if a situation doesn't seem good, He is a master at making beauty from ashes and joy spring forth from mourning.

God not only completes, He perfects. Hebrews 12:2 says, "Fixing our eyes on Jesus, the pioneer and perfecter of our faith." When He finishes, He creates a brilliant masterpiece! There have been seasons of my life where I have asked, "How is God going to make this good?" It is against His goodness to leave things undone. When we submit our lives to Him, He starts, completes, and makes it beautiful! Fix your eyes on Jesus, not on the situation or the emotions of the situation; stay focused on Him! While God is doing His finest work, your job is to trust and obey. Don't try to take things into your own hands. We make a mess when we try to control and fix things in our strength! Discern what God is asking you to do and do it. Maybe that means forgiveness or repentance. Perhaps that means taking a step of faith to start something new. Whatever it is, He knows your end and your beginning. He will guide you into His goodness.

Be encouraged today. He is Good, and He is God. He is working all things together for your good and for His glory! Yield to His goodness, knowing that He finishes what He starts! The best chapters of your story have yet to be revealed. Stay in faith; don't stop reading before it gets good. He is a much better story writer than we are!

— A DECLARATION FOR TODAY —

My best day is today, and my path only gets brighter and brighter!

Allow your faith to be stirred today! Take a minute and journal your gratitude for the good things God is doing.

_____

_____

_____

_____

_____

_____

_____

_____

_____

_____

_____

_____

"Death and life are in the power of the tongue and those
who love it will eat its fruit."
Proverbs 18:21 ESV

Day 24

Do you remember the old quip, you are what you eat? This takes me back to when my kids decided to give up fast food. We recently found an old paper my daughter wrote about me for Mother's Day one year. She boasted that I hardly ever let them eat fast food. Then something happened... she became a teenager with a driver's license. Suddenly, the homemade meals she had loved as a child weren't hitting the spot. In fact, at one point, the majority of her paychecks were going to fast food. Not too long ago, my teenagers decided to eat healthily. They were determined to ditch fast food once and for all. This decision sounded very doable at the moment. The problem came the next day after school when they were hungry and craving greasy delicacies. They caved, yet they were frustrated that they didn't look or feel any better. They wanted to have their fries and eat them, too (lol). Isn't that how we live our lives sometimes? We want to vent, complain, talk defeat, and still eat the fruit of a victorious, faith-filled confession. Proverbs 18:21 says, "Death and life are in the power of the tongue, and those who love it will eat its fruit." Basically, what you say creates what you get. You can't speak one way and expect a different outcome in your life.

"CHANGE YOUR TRAJECTORY BY
CHANGING YOUR CONFESSION!"

The Book of James likens the tongue to the utterance of a small ship with the ability to determine the entire course. Frustration occurs when we speak in alignment with our flesh yet expect spiritual results. This is no different from my children, who eat to satisfy their cravings and expect to have a healthy and fit body.

Your words hold the power. Think of it this way: your confession, whether positive or negative, faith-filled or doubt-ridden, is either putting an "amen" on truth or lies in your life. The word "amen"– what we say at the end of prayers or in the middle of a good sermon– is a word of agreement. Amen means, "Let it be so." What are you using your confession to say, let it be so too Are you believing and agreeing with the lies of the enemy for your life by speaking fear and negativity? Are you agreeing with your own thoughts of self-doubt? Or are you declaring, let it be to God's plans to prosper you, to give you life and life abundantly? What you speak matters. If you don't like where your life is, think about the words you have been speaking. Change your trajectory by changing your confession! You are what you speak; start declaring what God says about you!

I declare and confess what the Word of God says about me!

Journal:

What are the areas you are most frustrated by? Make a list of faith-filled declarations over those areas.

_____

_____

_____

_____

_____

_____

_____

_____

_____

_____

_____

_____

Day 25

Seven years ago, we moved from a lovely neighborhood of newly built houses to an old farmhouse. One of the motivating factors for our move was to have a little more privacy. While raising our kids in a neighborhood was fun, we began to crave our space and boundaries. There were always kids in our yard and the doorbell was always ringing. Once we made the move, we were so grateful for the space and privacy. One day, I noticed our garbage was strung all over the yard. This began to happen regularly. With a bit of watchfulness, I realized the neighbor's dogs were getting into my garbage and going to the bathroom in our yard. If that weren't enough, they'd bark at us on our own property. The whole reason we moved to the country was to have our space be our space. I became bothered by our space not being respected. I had to decide on what I would tolerate on my property. I eventually had to shoo the dogs away until they stopped coming to our yard, and I reminded them it was not their domain to rule on. This incident reminded me of our responsibility in life. Colossians 4:2 says, "Devote yourself to prayer; be watchful and thankful." I want to focus on the words watchful and thankful. In life, we need to take responsibility to watch over the affairs of our household.

— "STAND UP FOR WHAT IS YOURS BY FAITH." —

If something is happening in my house with my children, myself, or my husband, I am responsible for praying and drawing a boundary line for the enemy. The Bible tells us in John 10:10 that the enemy's plan for us is to kill, steal, and destroy. He will do whatever it takes to start messing with what is yours! Be watchful in prayer. Don't wait for things to erupt. Ask God to show you where the enemy is trying to get into your life at seed level. It could be an attitude from a child or simply a small compromise here or there. Take authority over what is yours! Set a boundary line in your life. The enemy can't just cause havoc in your home unless you allow it. Stand firm in faith. If there are areas where He has tried to take dominion, reestablish what is yours through prayer!

The second word that sticks out to me in Colossians 4 is thankfulness. Gratitude guards our hearts and keeps us alert. When we moved, I was so thankful for space that it bothered me even more when unwanted dogs tried to take what was mine. Gratitude for what God is doing in your life causes you to be even more protective. When you are thankful for your spouse and children, you will get mad when the enemy tries to disrupt what you know God has established! Stand up for what is yours by faith. Stay grateful for what God has given you. Thank Him for the unity, peace, and love in your home. Thank God for a house that loves and fears the Lord. Be watchful and take responsibility to kick the enemy out of what God has established as yours!

— A DECLARATION FOR TODAY —

The enemy cannot have an inch of the territory God has given me in my life!

Journal:

Make an assessment today of what God has established as yours. Are there areas the enemy has tried to sneak and take ground?

_____

_____

_____

_____

_____

_____

_____

_____

_____

_____

_____

_____

_____

"Watch and pray so that you will not fall into temptation. The spirit is willing, but the flesh is weak."
Matthew 26:41 NIV

Day 26

We have a joke in our family that when it comes to food, I am a temptress. I eat very healthily, but there is always some sort of baked good presented beautifully on our island in the kitchen. My family is always on me for going against their health goals while I stick to mine. My motivation is that I love them, so I try to make things they like...although they don't see it that way (yet they partake anyway)! Certain snacks I put out they walk by and not even desire, but then there are the favorites like cupcakes and almond torte. My rebuttal is always that I'm helping them work on self-discipline (lol). Oftentimes, I will quote Matthew 26:41 to them as a joke, "The spirit is willing, but the flesh is weak."

Not that I liken myself to the adversary of our souls, but this principle of temptation applies to our lives. The Bible reminds us that one of the greatest traits of the enemy is his craftiness. The devil is not creative, but he sure is deceitful. He knows exactly which temptations you could pass by and the ones that cause you to stop and indulge. His goal is to trip us up and entangle us with sin. Matthew 26:41 tells us to stay diligent, watch and pray, assess our lives continually, and allow the Holy Spirit to search our hearts.

"BE WATCHFUL; THE SPIRIT IN YOU ALWAYS EMPOWERS YOU TO OVERCOME TEMPTATION!"

The devil's craftiness usually manifests in small ways rather than obvious destruction. Faith starts as a seed, and so does sin. Many situations we have overcome that cause us to grow as believers are not one-and-done things. We need to take an ongoing account of our lives. Are there areas you once overcame, but now you have let your guard down? Just a little bit of compromise causes us to lose ground in our faith. The enemy doesn't want you to progress. He wants to trip you up and hold you back. The spirit is willing, but the flesh is weak. Our spirits want to do what is right, and we want to grow in God, but there is a continual battle that we will always have with our flesh. The Apostle Paul talks about this ongoing battle in Romans 7:15. He gives us a glimpse into the temptation of his flesh when he says, "What I want to do I do not do, but what I hate to do." In verse 17, he says, "It is no longer myself who do it; but it is the sin living in me."

So, if this is an ongoing battle, how do we overcome it? By watching carefully over our lives. Ask the Holy Spirit to show you any areas that may be trying to trip you up. Be alert to your weaknesses, the things that tempt you. Maybe it's gossip or unforgiveness. Whatever it is, kill it in seed form! Remember, the Bible tells us that our temptation comes from one of two places– the enemy of our souls or our own evil desires. Be watchful. The spirit in you always empowers you to overcome temptation!

— A DECLARATION FOR TODAY —————————

I will diligently watch and pray, allowing the Holy Spirit to purify my heart.

Journal:

The enemy is repetitive. What are some patterns you can recognize where he tries to trip you up? What desires cause you to be prone to temptation? Be aware, diligent, and prayed up!

_____

_____

_____

_____

_____

_____

_____

_____

_____

_____

_____

_____

_____

"Finally, brothers and sisters, whatever is true, whatever is noble, whatever is right, whatever is pure, whatever is lovely, whatever is admirable- if anything is excellent or praiseworthy-think about such things."
Philippians 4:8 NIV

Day 27

Often, in a car ride, if there is a prolonged silence, my husband will turn and ask me what I am thinking. He is curious about what is occupying my mind. At that moment, I realized that I didn't even recognize the silence because of the full conversation that had been taking place inside my head. I am a classic overthinker. My thoughts are like tabs open on a computer or cell phone. They can range from simple task lists to deep thoughts and intense conversations. I would venture to say that I am not the only overthinker out there. God makes most women as complex thinkers (and great multi-taskers, too!) The ability to think this way is a gift from God. However, it can also become a burden if we don't steward it correctly. If we liken our mind to a computer, the open tabs often lead to a low battery. I can't tell you how many times my phone battery has run low in times of need. At this moment, one of my kids typically grabs my phone and closes about a dozen open tabs. Many open tabs drain batteries, and unbridled complex thinking can drain us emotionally and spiritually.

The Apostle Paul speaks often in his letters to the churches about taking account of your thoughts.

"MEDITATE ON GOOD THINGS, ENVISIONING A LIFE OF GOD'S BEST."

In Philippians 4:6, Paul commands believers not to be anxious but to present their requests to God in prayer and thanksgiving, recognizing the correlation between our continual thoughts (especially us overthinkers) and anxiety. Racing thoughts can take us outside of God's grace. A simple to-do list in our minds can send us into a full-blown panic attack if we allow it to. Paul is very forthright in his instruction on anxious thinking. He commands us *not* to be anxious. This reminds me that this is an area you *can* control. How can these beautifully complex, overthinking brains control thoughts that lead to anxiety? First, Paul tells us in Philippians 4:4-5 to give thanks to God in everything and to take our worries to Him in prayer- nothing realigns our thinking more. We often stop at verses 4-6, but verse 8 is the key to lasting soundness of the mind. Philippians 4:8 reminds us to think about whatever is true, noble, right, pure, lovely, admirable, excellent, and praiseworthy. This is the key to taming our complex thinking! How would your thinking would be different based on these standards alone? Instead of meditating on lies or negativity, meditate on good things, envisioning a life of God's best. Paul then tells us that this type of thinking will yield clarity. We will be able to know and discern the will of God. I don't know about you, but I want that type of thinking. I want clarity rather than confusion and peace rather than strife and chaos in my thinking! Set your mind in a new direction of thinking, as in Philippians 4:6, and you will have peace, joy, and clarity like never before!

— A DECLARATION FOR TODAY ————————

I will take control over what occupies my mind, setting my mind on things above.

Journal:

Studies show that we mull over the same 3-4 thoughts all day in different ways. Try keeping track of the 3-4 thoughts you think about each day. How do they measure up to Paul's standard of thinking?

Day 28

Have you ever encountered a stubborn animal? We have a French Bulldog named Louie. Louie is as sweet as can be except in the morning. To my surprise, when I would wake Louie up to go outside, he would snarl at me. He would refuse to budge. Many mornings, it feels like Louie is one of my teenagers who I'm telling to get up for school. If Louie is still sleepy, he won't budge. While stubbornness is often a negative attribute (in teenagers and bulldogs), there are some good sides to being stubborn. Oxford Dictionary defines stubbornness as "determination not to change one's attitude or position on something, especially despite good arguments or reasons to do so." I love the last part of that definition, "Especially despite." A stubborn person has their mind made up. They are unshaken and immovable by other opinions or circumstances that should cause them to change their mind.

As Christians, we need to be stubborn about God's things. We are often stubborn about our own likes, opinions, and preferences, but we give in too easily when life or the enemy offers us "good arguments or reasons to change our mind."

"WHEN YOU HAVE DONE EVERYTHING ELSE, KEEP STANDING IN FAITH!"

Ephesians 6:13 tells us to be stubborn when it comes to our faith, "Therefore take up the whole armor of God, that you may be able to withstand in the evil day, and having done all, to stand firm." The Bible admonishes us to "stand firm"– to become immovable when it comes to our faith.

A stubborn person doesn't conform their will to the environment around them. Their mind is made up, and they cannot be pressed even when challenged. When our human will aligns with God's will, we become unstoppable!

Set your mind to believe God. Don't give in to fear, worry, sin, or discouragement! You have the armor of God. You have the helmet of salvation, the shield of faith, the breastplate of righteousness, the sword of the spirit, the shoes of peace. Dig those shoes down deep on the soil of faith and stand ready! Stubborn is your new normal!

Make a decision today to be bulldog stubborn and see God's best come to pass in your life. When you have done everything else, keep standing in faith!

— A DECLARATION FOR TODAY —————————

Quitting is not an option. Nothing is impossible with God!

Repent of any unbelief. Write a prayer of dedication to be more steadfast than ever about the things of God!

_____

_____

_____

_____

_____

_____

_____

_____

_____

_____

_____

Day 29

There is no conversation I hate worse having with my husband than on budget day. Budget day is when we sit down and review each transaction that has left our bank account.

Yikes... the purchases that seemed so rational at the moment all of a sudden make me question my ability to make decisions at all. Then there are the moments when I realized I had made some good decisions. Wow, am I proud of those moments! There's something about accountability that causes you to live differently, more wisely, and much more calculated! Romans 14:12 tells us that there is a conversation we will have with God one day that will make budget day feel like a picnic. This conversation is an account of how we have stewarded our lives before God. This conversation will be a one-on-one conversation.

I can't begin to imagine the moment when I, the created, am standing before my Creator, going over an itemized scroll of how I spent my life. How will you feel in that moment?

"WHEN GOD CREATED YOU, HE CREATED YOU WITH A PURPOSE IN ALIGNMENT WITH YOUR POTENTIAL, NOT YOUR LIMITATIONS."

What would you want your response to be if you imagined yourself in that position? What excuses would you come up with that seemed logical in the moment yet so empty before your Creator?

Spend a moment there. How do you see your life in light of the potential of the one who formed you and placed gifts, callings, destinies, and assignments aside for you?

Do you see greater things you knew you were purposed for but were too afraid to accomplish? When God created you, He created you with a purpose in alignment with your potential, not your limitations. He looks at you today in that same light, full of purpose and potential both given by and empowered by Him.

Start today living from a Romans 12:14 moment. What do I want the account that I give God to be? Start living that life today! Remember, "You can do *all* things through Christ who gives you strength." (Phil 4:13).

— A DECLARATION FOR TODAY —

I live from a Romans 12:14 moment. My life will be a good account to God!

Journal:

Take a moment and journal the account you would want to bring before God.

_____

_____

_____

_____

_____

_____

_____

_____

_____

_____

_____

"The word of the Lord came to me: 'What do you see Jeremiah?' 'I see the branch of an almond tree,' I replied. The Lord said to me, 'You have seen correctly, for I am watching over my word to see that it is fulfilled.'"
Jeremiah 1:11-12 NIV

Day 30

There are two conditions that I hate driving in: snow and fog. As I mentioned before, there was a time that I hit fog so thick that I had zero visibility as I headed to a lacrosse tournament. I was literally driving by faith, not sight! I had to use the little I had to guide me on my path, in this case, the faint tail lights of the car in front of me. The fog was so thick that I couldn't even pull to the side of the road because I had no clue what was on my left or right. The lesson I learned that day was how scary it was to move forward without sight. (And as you can tell, the story stayed with me for many life lessons!)

Living life without seeing what is ahead can be equally daunting. God doesn't want you to live in a perpetual state of wandering around or paralyzed from moving forward due to fear. As His children, God has given us the beautiful gift of perception. The Oxford Dictionary defines perception as "The ability to see, hear or become aware of something through the senses." By spiritual definition, perception is the ability to see, hear, or become aware of something by your spirit. If positioned from a place of prayer, nothing God does in your life should surprise or shock you.

"GOD SPEAKS, WE HEAR AND OBEY, AND GOD SEES IT TO COMPLETION."

Jeremiah 1:11-12 reads, "The word of the Lord came to me: 'What do you see Jeremiah?' 'I see the branch of an almond tree,' I replied. The Lord said to me, 'You have seen correctly, for I am watching over my word to see that it is fulfilled.'" In this scripture, God asked Jeremiah what he saw. Jeremiah just asked God for direction. Instead of giving Jeremiah a vocal response–which I think we all would prefer (an audible voice from heaven would take much of the guesswork out of hearing from God)– God asks Jeremiah what he sees. God wanted Jeremiah to lean in and see by the spirit what God was speaking. As Jeremiah responded to God, God assured him, "I will watch over that word to see it come to pass." What a beautiful picture of how perception works. God speaks, we hear and obey, and God sees it to completion.

There will be seasons of your life when you hear God loud and clear. There will be other seasons where you feel like you are driving through dense fog. Whichever season you are in, lean in to hear His voice. Ask God for guidance and direction. The Bible says, "His Word is a lamp to my feet and a light to my path" (Psalm 119: 105).

He wants to speak to you. Will you take time to perceive what He is saying? As you perceive, God will prepare you for what He wants to perform in your life! Set your spiritual perception on high and get ready for lots of thanksgiving as God delivers on what He has spoken to you!

— A DECLARATION FOR TODAY

My path gets brighter and brighter.

Journal:

As Jeremiah took time to perceive what God was saying, take time to perceive what God is speaking to you. What do you see?

_____

_____

_____

_____

_____

_____

_____

_____

_____

_____

_____

_____

"OCCUPY UNTIL I COME."

Luke 19:13
KJV

ABOUT THE AUTHOR

Joie Miller is passionate about encouraging women to understand who they are in Christ and to see them connect with their God-given purpose so they can walk in victory. She is the host of The Joie Miller Podcast and the pastor of Elle Women's Ministry. She loves to connect with women through her different mentorship platforms. She has previously released *Masterpiece*, a six-week Bible study, *Bold: A 30-Day Devotion*, *Rooted*, and *The Joie Miller Planner*.

Pastor Joie has been married to her high school sweetheart, Pastor Nathan Miller, for almost 25 years. Together, they pastor Champion Christian Center in the Pittsburgh area. She is also the mother of six wonderful children: Evan and bonus daughter Ellionna, Addison, Ava, Maddox, and Mia. She is also the proud grandmother of Eveleigh.

For more information on Pastor Joie's ministries, to purchase her other products, or to contact her for bookings, check out www.joiemiller.co